A Crabtree Roots Book

It's Thanksgiving!

My Favorite Holiday

AMY CULLIFORD

CRABTREE
Publishing Company
www.crabtreebooks.com

School-to-Home Support for Caregivers and Teachers

This book helps children grow by letting them practice reading. Here are a few guiding questions to help the reader build his or her comprehension skills. Possible answers appear here in red.

Before Reading:

- What do I think this book is about?
    - *I think this book is about Thanksgiving.*
    - *I think this book is about the food we eat at Thanksgiving dinner.*
- What do I want to learn about this topic?
    - *I want to learn more about turkeys at Thanksgiving.*
    - *I want to learn why this holiday is called Thanksgiving.*

During Reading:

- I wonder why...
    - *I wonder why turkeys are the meat we eat on Thanksgiving.*
    - *I wonder why there are parades on Thanksgiving.*
- What have I learned so far?
    - *I have learned that there is usually a pie after dinner on Thanksgiving.*
    - *I have learned that many people play football on Thanksgiving.*

After Reading:

- What details did I learn about this topic?
    - *I have learned that we all give thanks on Thanksgiving.*
    - *I have learned that we eat delicious food on Thanksgiving.*
- Read the book again and look for the vocabulary words.
    - *I see the word **parade** on page 10 and the word **football** on page 13. The other vocabulary words are found on page 14.*

It is **Thanksgiving** Day!

We all give thanks.

We eat **turkey**.

We also eat **pie**! Yum!

I see a **parade**.

macy's
PARK
PARK
LOVE WHERE YOU LEASE
CELLULAR EXPRESS
TROLLBEADS
PRET A MANGER

We play **football**.

Word List

Sight Words

a
all
also
day
eat
give
I
is
it
play
see
thanks
we
yum

Words to Know

football

parade

pie

Thanksgiving

turkey

23 Words

It is **Thanksgiving** Day!

We all give thanks.

We eat **turkey**.

We also eat **pie**! Yum!

I see a **parade**.

We play **football**.

CRABTREE
Publishing Company

It's Thanksgiving!

My Favorite Holiday

Written by: Amy Culliford
Designed by: Bobbie Houser
Series Development: James Earley
Proofreader: Petrice Custance
Educational Consultant: Marie Lemke M.Ed.
Photographs:
Shutterstock: NYC Russ: cover; Rawpixel.com: p. 1; Monkey Business Images: p. 3, 14; Roman Samborskyi: p. 5, 7, 14; LightField Studios: p. 8, 14; a katz: p. 10-11, 14; sirtravelalot: p. 12, 14

Library and Archives Canada Cataloguing in Publication

CIP available at Library and Archives Canada

Library of Congress Cataloging-in-Publication Data

CIP available at Library of Congress

Crabtree Publishing Company

www.crabtreebooks.com 1-800-387-7650

Printed in the USA/072022/CG20220201

 In Canada: We acknowledge the financial support of the Government of Canada through the Canada Book Fund for our publishing activities.

Published in the United States
Crabtree Publishing
347 Fifth Avenue, Suite 1402-145
New York, NY, 10016

Published in Canada
Crabtree Publishing
616 Welland Ave.
St. Catharines, ON, L2M 5V6